FROM NOTHING

TO SOMETHING.

THE STORY OF MY LIFE

TAMIKA MCCLAIN

Tina

Thank you
For your love
and Support

Tamika McClain

Copyright © 2018 Tamika McClain

McClain Publishing Group

Cleveland, OH

ISBN-13: 978-0-692-16530-0

Printed in the United States of America

Table of Contents

INTRODUCTION

All my life people used me, hurt me, lied to me, bullied me, and talked about me. But someone special name Ethel Banks told me, "Pearls of wisdom is worth more than rubies". Timeless truths that if allowed to sink in hold secrets of living genuinely, joyfully, generously and honestly.

As a child I've had lots of pain and stumbling blocks in my life. I didn't feel loved and I didn't feel wanted. Growing up as a child all I knew was darkness and pain. I never knew love and light. I remembered I had to pretend like I had a happy life. Growing up was a struggle and a challenge for me. It seemed like I was alone in the dark and couldn't find a way out.

Being a victim of such unfortunate experiences, such as being homeless, into hard drugs, victimized and abused sexually, physically abused, and several other misfortunes inspired me to set out and give back to my community in ways I felt led.

But God! He has a way of fixing everything by bringing people into your life that truly means something to you and sometimes even people that shouldn't be there. It was my job to find out the difference. First, I had to find out and learn how to love myself. And secondly, I had to forgive all the people that brought pain into my life. As you take this journey through this book you will discover how I went from NOTHING TO SOMETHING.

I wrote this book to share with you my life story in hopes that it will help save and change your circumstances, and encourage and inspire you to greater heights. Know that there is nothing you can't overcome, to reach your goal and live life to its fullest potential.

CHAPTER 1

IN THE BEGINNING

When most people reminisce about their childhood, the memories are usually exciting, for some others, it is bittersweet, having a blend of both exciting and not so exciting times. But mine was neither exciting nor bittersweet; my childhood was marred and scarred by abandonment, pain, abuse, tears, and despair. Before I knew my name, I knew all about pain, before I could learn to read, I knew how to read the handwriting of abuse. Even though it's been two score years, my memory serves me well and I remember certain events photographically, and others were narrated to me as I grew older.

I vaguely remember many nights my older siblings, Nita, Anthony and I spent alone in the tiny studio apartment that was gloomy and dirtier than a pigsty. Although my mother was a tidy woman, the apartment was usually very unkempt when she was in her zone of drunkenness and sex. We were all so young but will stay in the house hungry and will cry all night till we slept on empty stomachs and dried flaky tears on our cheeks. The responsibility always fell on Nita who was the oldest to try and make some sense of our life. But how much could a young 8-year-old do? My mother will leave us home hungry to go to the bar to get drunk, then she'll return in the dead of the night drunk as a skunk and with random men. So even when I really didn't understand what was happening at the time, I realize that one of the earliest sounds I was accustomed to was the sound of These random men would come into our shabby house with my mother and will have wild sex until they both passed out. She didn't even care that she had her children in the same room. Maybe she thought we were too young to know anything, but how wrong she was. She was more interested in getting drunk and having sex with random men than she was in looking after her children.

Although I was the youngest of the children, I still remember these different events just like they just happened yesterday. Never underestimate the memory of a child, the mind has a way of playing back memories that as the child gets older, all the things that happened begin to have an interpretation, the childhood experiences begin to make sense. So you can only lie to a child but for a while, as the child grows older, the child gains clarity. Children assimilate everything going on and it is stored somewhere in their minds for later interpretation.

Till this day, I'm aware and feel the pain of my past. My sad life began the moment I came into the world, born into a dysfunctional home, Sometimes I wonder what my parents were doing having children they had no means, and experience nor desire for. When I was just about 12 months old, my mother, detesting me so much, and craving her wild nights so much decided to put me in a trash bag outside the bar and went into the bar to drink and wallow in lasciviousness. She didn't want me; I must have been a disturbance to her so much that she believed her life would be better off without me. She literally wanted me to die in the trash. Now she could have given me up for adoption, but she chose to just abandon me in the same place where people threw things that were rotten, wasted or unwanted in. To her, I was only as useful as garbage.

I still struggle with trying to understand and make sense of the rationale behind her action. Why would a Mother toss away a baby that grew inside her for 9 months like an orange peel? An innocent baby who knew nothing and did nothing. This affected my self-esteem and self-perception later in life. My thinking was pretty basic, if the woman who gave birth to me considered me worthless, useless and garbage, who was I, or anyone else for that matter to think anything better of me. Even when I received compliments, I always took them as lies and nothing but sheer patronage, or that the compliments came with a price I was going to somehow have to pay.

But it is by the mercies of the Lord that I can even sit here at my desk and write this book, just like the scripture says in the book of Lamentations.

"Because of the LORD's great love, we are not consumed,

For his compassions never fail."

Lam 3:22

Yes, his compassions never fail, and that is why I am alive today. My innocent cries from the trash attracted two ladies who stayed down the street from the bar. Their names were Ethel and Linda. According to their account, what they heard was probably my last desperate cry for help, because I was already pale and turning purple. They took me out of the trash bag and wrapped me in what extra clothing they had, as my small frame was cold as ice. In a frenzy, they tried all they could to resuscitate me, and, by God's great love, I wasn't consumed by that trash can that almost snuffed the life out of me. These women were the angels the Lord used to preserve my life, even when I knew nothing, even when I wasn't self-aware, God protected me, and preserved me for a purpose. To this day, I look back and thank God for them.

Ethel was Linda's Mother, and she took me in as one of

her own children. And Linda loved me like her own sister. Ethel was a good woman and was a good mother to me. She took on the responsibility of raising a child she picked from the trash, she once told me many years later that she never had a doubt in her heart it was the right thing to do. As soon as she heard that cry, she knew she had to do something, as something on the inside of her stirred, and after she did some investigating and realized who my mother was, she knew if she returned me back to her at that time, I was probably going to end up back in that trash, and who knows if I'd be lucky the second time. What Ethel did for me was even more amazing because she was in a very rough place in her life financially, and really couldn't add the burden of a child to it, but she did, even when her relatives told her it was a foolish thing to do at the time. She stuck to her guns and did everything she could to take care of me. Ethel was strict and didn't allow me to get away with so much, she truly cared about me and did all she could to raise me the right way, she was disciplined yet loving.

Linda was like a second mother and older sister to me, she

also loved me like I was really a biological part of their family.

I don't know how I found out so early, but somehow I learned that Ethel was not my real Mother, I started to always ask Ethel, "Where's my Mommy? I want my Mommy." But my Mother Cece was still the same woman she was when she dropped me in that trash and left me to die. In retrospect, I wonder what I really was looking for, when I had a woman who loved me like her own and took me in from the trash and nursed me to health, provided for me, disciplined me and brought me up. My little mind didn't know better at the time.

***

When I was six years old, my biological mother, Cece came to Ethel's house. She had been inquiring around, and word in the hood had it that Ethel had picked up a baby from the trash. But I wonder why or how she waited for so many years to even show up and remembered she had a baby. But this was a baby she wanted dead, a baby that she left to die out there in the cold and in the trash. How come she felt no shame in coming out and even owning up to being the mother who trashed her baby of just 12 months old?

But she was still the same woman, she was still a drunk. She came and demanded that Ethel give me over to her. Ethel had known my Mother from around town, but she never knew that she was the Mother of the baby she had picked from the trash, the baby she had cared and loved like hers for 5 years. Ethel was beyond shocked, as she had never imagined that it was Cece who did something as awful as throw a baby away. They argued back and forth. Ethel remained resolute that she had no rights to a baby she trashed like waste. It didn't even help that Cece was reeking of alcohol, and her movement impaired by alcohol.

"You have no right to come here and look for a baby you left for dead 5 years ago. You must be the worst mother on earth to do that, and you dare stand before me as drunk as you are asking to have your baby back. You ought to be ashamed Cece. Cover your face in shame!" Ethel told her.

"Ethel, give me my baby, the child is mine, and I knew someone was going to take care of her. I made a mistake, but I'm back now, I'd always known that the baby was with you. I want my baby! Give me my baby!" My Mom retorted. I stood right there behind Ethel as tears escaped my eyes. I wanted my Mom, I just wanted her.

"You better leave my front porch before I call the police and tell them there's a drunken woman disturbing the peace of me and my family right now!" Ethel threatened.

"I'll be back," Cece promised, "I won't back off until you give me my baby."

That was the first of many visits Cece paid to Ethel's house. Sometimes she would show up with black eyes looking all beat up, having been in fights with men, men that abused her constantly. Even as a young 6-year-old child, it hurt me to see my Mom that way, blood they say is thicker than water. I always pitied her and wanted to be with her, not minding what she was like or how irresponsible she was. My Dad came with her one day, and somehow, Ethel bowed to the pressure and because I wanted it too, she allowed me to go and spend some time with them. I was young and naïve, what did I know, I was probably just driven by the blood in me. But they refused to return me to Ethel after 6 months; they only did after Ethel threatened to call the police.

I got a glimpse of the kind of life my Mother lived during the time I spent with her, one time she had jumped out the window from the fourth floor in a high-rise building as she was running away from one of her abusive boyfriends who was beating her. She was badly injured in the fall; her days were full of pain and so much abuse I felt for her. She seemed to have a penchant for choosing strange men. All the men she had relations with including my father abused her immensely. Soon the abuse was spilling over to me, one time I was playing by myself in the living room when one of her boyfriend's came and started choking and strangling me, I couldn't breathe, I was almost losing it, just before my Mom came in and he stopped after she confronted him. I honestly wonder what strange demon took over the mind of that man who tried to kill me. She never got along with my Dad, and I still wonder what their union was about in the first place. They argued so much, it always ended with my Dad beating her. One time he beat her with a baseball bat.

***

Growing up with so much dysfunction had its toll on my young mind, and the bad things that happened didn't help either. The dark cloud hung over my life for a very long time. Just before I turned 8 years old, I was raped for the first time. I was raped severally and so severely that I found it a norm, it felt like a very regular occurrence at the time.

Ethel used to deal in drugs, all kinds of drugs, heroin, weed, crack, etc., and she had different men always coming around the house to buy from her. One of the men took particular interest in me, and he would hand me $5 bills and ask me to go buy candy at the store by the corner of the street. One day he asked me to come and sit on his lap, and I innocently did so. After all, this was the man who always gave me money to buy candy. While I sat on his leg, I felt him lick me with his mouth lightly nibbling my ear, and I would be tickled and laugh, and try to avoid his mouth, but soon I began to feel a certain pressure against my little bum as I sat on his laps, I didn't understand what was happening. Nothing was poking me when I first sat on his lap, I wondered what was now making me uncomfortable there.

This continued for a while until one day, he lifted my skirt and stuck one finger up my private area. I whimpered at the intrusion, I hadn't been expecting anything of the kind. He took out the finger, it was his middle finger, and he smelt it, and then licked it.

"Gosh, you taste and smell so good! Whoever finally has you will be so lucky," he exclaimed as I hurriedly eased off him and ran away.

One of Linda's friends had a boyfriend I used to babysit for, he also abused me. Whenever he would return home, and I was attempting to leave, he would follow me to the door, the door he had already locked. Right there at the door, he would expose himself and make me go on my knees and pleasure him orally. It was then I realized what it was that always poked my but whenever I sat on the other man's lap, it was this appendage between his legs.

He would make me touch him and suck him until he shot his goo up on my face. Other times, he will ask me to undress and he'll also stick his fingers into me. It hurt so much, but I endured the pain. He would then threaten me not to tell anyone. Naïve and scared, I wouldn't tell anyone, I was going to keep the secret because somehow, I felt like I was the one at fault, I must have done something wrong.

Maybe the most shocking of my abusers was Raymond, who was like a grandfather to me. He was the father of Ethel's kids. He grabbed me one day when Ethel went to the store, leaving just both of us in the house. He would lubricate himself lavishly with cooking oil and then force himself into me. It was really painful. Some other times, he would just make me watch him masturbate himself with his strange choice of lubrication until he had an orgasm. He also threatened to hurt me if I mentioned a word of what he did to me to anyone. And I was obedient, how could I tell anyone. I felt the fault was mine.

Ethel was going to the store on this fateful day, and I could see it was just he and my cousin in the house.

"Ethel, please I want to go with you, please take me with you, I don't want to stay at home, please," I begged her.

"Oh, come on darling, don't worry, I won't be long, and don't worry, Raymond will take care of you until I come back," she looked at Raymond who was sitting on a couch nearby, "Isn't that right Raymond?" she asked him.

"Oh, yes, of course, you know I'll take care of her," he said to Ethel but looking at me with evil eyes. I could tell that he was going to pounce on me right after Ethel had left.

Ethel kissed me on both my cheeks. "So, I gotta run now, I'll soon be back, and I'll get you something on my way back."

As soon as she left, he sent my cousin on some really useless errand, and this time it was fish grease he found handy. While he was lubricating himself and with a big lewd smile on his face, I made a beeline to escape from him, but he caught me, and slammed me on the bed, ready to really force his way into me. Thankfully, my cousin walked into the room and that was my saving grace that day!

I dealt with the emotional turmoil of being raped severally by different men at various times. And it was worse that I blamed myself, I don't know how that came to be, but somehow, I felt like it was my fault these men were doing this to me. Looking at the way my life started and all, I felt totally unwanted and rejected. At this time, I already knew my Mom once threw me in the trash, and that's where Ethel found me. Again, I thought that had to be my fault, even my mother didn't want me, and tried to throw me away, so these men too probably saw something hideous in me and decided to hurt me as a result.

Everything just pointed to the fact that it was all my doing, and I better endure it because it was my punishment in a way. My fingers were pointing back at myself. I was unloved, unwanted and now abuse was a punishment added to me. At a point, I became so used to being abused that if a day passes and I was not abused, I would wonder why no one had attempted to do it. I know for a fact that there are a bunch of young girls going through something similar right now, and my most important advice is for you to NOT believe it's your fault. Forget what your abuser the rapist says, forget what the society dictates, I hear some people argue that women who get raped because they were dressed 'provocatively' had it coming. I've never heard anything lamer. Nothing could be farther from the truth. So please, know that it is not your fault, and don't keep quiet about it, the more you stay silent, the harder it is to speak up, don't fall into that trap.

CHAPTER 2

WHEN ABNORMAL BECOMES NORMAL

Day to day I dealt with the emotions of being raped several times. That devastating repetition of this inhumane act that men did towards me caused me to become suicidal and to start to act out in other ways as an outlet.

When I was eight years old, I began to sell drugs, and this continued until I was about 16 years old. I sold just about everything, heroin, weed, cocaine, you name it; I had access to it and sold it. At ten years old, was when I became more curious about what the level of high was that these drugs could get you. I soon began to explore these drugs that people seem to die to get. I had my first puff of weed at 10 years old and boy did that weed take my mind places. Weed was in vogue, and everyone seemed to be doing it, so I gave it a try since I already peddled it. But it didn't take long for me to get hooked on it. I had smoked so much one day, but I was still going around looking for another joint, I had exhausted my supply. I came across a roach and I lit it. Now, don't think I smoked a cockroach. A roach was a term used to describe a small joint of weed that had already been smoked and thrown away. It was a popular slang in the 80's and 90's. I used to smoke in hiding, so Ethel and Linda had no idea that I had started using drugs at this time.

Another time, I came across a nice sized joint that had been left in the ashtray by Linda and her friends. I wonder what kind of joint it was because it sure did have a different feel and smell. After I smoked it, I was knocked out for about 16 hours. I didn't wake up till afternoon the next day. I could not believe it, I couldn't believe the time. I remember waking up with a strong urge to use the bathroom. But my mind was still in shambles, the effect of whatever I had smoked was still heavy on my mind. I ended up in the kitchen instead of the bathroom; my high mind imagined the trash can was the toilet seat.

Ethel walked in just as I was urinating in the trash can, "Tamika, what is wrong with you? Are you out of your mind?"

"Nothing is wrong," I managed to reply in the best voice I could find.

"Then why are you easing yourself in the trash can?" She shouted, and came close to me, "and why are your eyes so red?"

Until Ethel mentioned that I was easing myself in the trash can, I had no idea that was the case; I imagined I was in the bathroom. But then it dawned on me altogether, I was high as a skunk even after 16 hours of being passed out.

Linda must have heard Ethel shouting at me, so she came into the kitchen as well.

"Mom, can't you see Tamika is high? She's been smoking weed in this house, and she's been stealing it too."

"What!" Ethel exclaimed, "Is that so, Tamika? You've been smoking weed?"

My fucked-up self had no answer, I could barely even mouth the words I wanted to say, I was going to say I was sorry, but nothing came out. I just sat there on the trash looking from Ethel to Linda and back to Ethel, then down at myself, still wondering what I was thinking, taking a piss in the trash. I won't forget that night because I was severely disciplined until the entire highness left me, I was disciplined to the third degree. It was at times like this that my childish mind would miss my birth mother. Well, more like I missed the idea of her.

I felt sorry for the woman she had become, and even with what had happened, I still loved her although it hurt for me to love her. I could not even pick up the phone to call her. I felt like an involuntary victim in my own life. On the one hand, I felt my past was holding me hostage and then, on the other hand, I was thankful for God allowing me to have a new family. I was clearly lost and fighting my own battles, which sometimes I appeared to be doing alone.

Just like clockwork when I turned ten, my biological mother returned asking for me again. This time around, she brought a social worker.

"My child is coming with me," she told Ethel.

I didn't want to go, but the social worker informed me that I had to go with Ce-ce.

"I'm not going anywhere," I told them."If you make me

go, I will kill myself!" This I truly meant. By this age, I had already been molested and raped. I knew that life would get a whole lot worse if I went with her and I didn't want that for myself.

"We will be back," the social worker said when she saw that I had made up my mind.

"Don't bother; there's no need to come back," I told them. My mind was already made up; I did not want to go with my mother.

Ce-Ce was a nice smart lady when she was sober, but she had a weakness, men. And not the good type of men, she had a penchant for terrible men and what was crazy was that she loved them more than me. Under her watch, some of the men she brought to the house started touching me. It wasn't like I didn't suffer the same fate at Ethel's, but I probably believed it might be different at Ce-ce's. But I could then see that Ethel's was better in different areas. It was awful and tough not having good parental guidance, I was alone and I soon started to feel depressed.

After all that had happened with my mother, I didn't have trust in anyone again. The woman who was supposed to protect me from harm had failed me too, who else could I trust? I was twelve when I had consensual sex for the first time; this was different from me being raped because I wanted this. I was scared to tell Ethel because I knew she would literally kill me, but she had no idea I had already been raped severally. This really was better than being raped, and I was choosing to make it happen myself. I kept my secrets to myself and went through each day with a heavy heart. Deep down I knew it was wrong, my conscience was not at peace, but it was the only way I felt accepted and wanted.

I was very young and dealt with so many issues. At my age, I ought to be free, but I was having a hard time. I had so many questions about my parents which I wanted answers for. I was just so confused and in turmoil. The more I kept on thinking, the more I felt angry I got enraged and wanted to lash out. Sex was my solace, and soon another vice joined in, stealing. All I wanted was a way to deal with the issues I had going on. I thought I was alone and nobody could understand me.

Like most young people of my age, I wanted to be famous. I wanted to go to Beverly Hills and live the good life that I saw on TV and in the magazines. I wanted to meet interesting people and open myself to new experiences. I decided to get into the flashy life I imagined getting into the porn industry. I was willing to take pictures in the nude, just to be a part of all that glitz and glamor.

My past molestation really took a toll on me; it started to make me become more sexual and aware of my body. I used to play hide and seek with the boys in the neighborhood. When they found me, I would let the boys fondle my breasts among other things. I would even purposely make noises so that they could find me; I really loved the attention.

All of this made me think that I was ready to have sex. I was only twelve, but I was already beginning to hump boys with my clothes on. In fourth grade I had several crushes on different boys; it was at this point that I began to have boyfriends.

My first boyfriend was Dwynne. We both went to Mary B. Martin on Hough together Dwynne was the first person I had desirable sex with. He was so funny and so serious at the same time but that's why I was so attracted to him. As we grew up, we lost contact and Dwynne moved to Cedar 105. He was not only a boyfriend he was my great friend also. Many years later, I ran into his sister, she dropped the bad news after I had asked her about him. She said "Tamika, Dwynne's gone." I said "gone where?" and that's when I found out that Dwynne had passed away, I was so heartbroken and couldn't believe it. Dwynne will forever be in my heart.

My next boyfriend was Dre; we met in Middle School, and also went to West Tech High School. I will never forget the day he asked me out. We started dating in our last year in middle school. Dre was a unique breed of a human, our relationship stood out from the others. Even if we were two different people, our blend was good. He was the ideal kind of boyfriend any young girl would want. He was a true gift. We would go everywhere together, and he never stressed me or made me sad, and quick to apologize when he was wrong. He never stressed me in any way, he sent me to class with a kiss and made sure I got back home afterward, if he couldn't walk me home, he would call to make sure I got home. Dre made me a very happy girl. A lot of girls wanted him, but he had eyes for only me. Dre was smart and handsome, I was his first kiss, and this was my first real feeling of love. I was his first love but not the first person he had sex with so when I found out that he had kids I couldn't believe it. I did love him, but somehow along the line, we just drifted apart, things were going too fast at home, and I was dealing with so much. We never broke up officially, we just drifted apart. I'm very protective of Dre, and I'm happy to still have him as a friend to this day. He remains an amazing man just like he had always been.

I met Ivan in the hood, and we really liked each other. Even though we were young, I believed we were in love; no one could tell me different. We always had a bond even when we were not together. He always respected and showed me love. We talked about everything, and then he went to jail. Yet, this didn't stop our love as he continued sending me letters. In his letters, he would write about how he missed and loved me and couldn't wait to be home with me. The letters begin to get sexual and in one letter he wrote that when he got home, he would do the 69 on me.

My brother Pookey found the letter lying on my dresser and confronted me with it. I had no idea what a 69 meant at that time. I thought Ivan wanted me to give him $69 which I didn't have. My brother told me it meant that Ivan wanted to go down on my private parts and wanted me to do the same to him as well. I did want him to do his part but not the other way around. Pookey was angry and told me that attitude wasn't me. I just told him to stop going through my stuff.

Eventually, Ivan was released from jail and came home to see me. He immediately began to kiss me, and it felt so good that I melted in his arms. He wanted me to have sex with him. This was going to be my second time willingly, and I allowed him. However, he wanted to do something new and he told me to bend over; he wanted to have sex doggie style. I admit that I enjoyed it.

Being with Ivan was good until I found out that he was a cheater. In addition to this, he was also very abusive. Once, he slapped me so hard that I fell to the floor. My face was blood red, and I began to cry because I had never been hit by a man before. He would tell me later that he loved me and that it was my fault one way or the other for him hitting me. I didn't learn until later in life that when a person hits you and then places the blame on everyone but himself, it's usually a sign that a person is abusive or have underlying anger issues. But with my severe past issues, I gave him another chance.

Even his mother loved me and wanted me to be with him, but he wasn't ready. He wanted me as well as other women too. He was my baby, but I discovered it was not true love. After several chances and a few new women, I fell down the line, I finally moved on. It was hard and painful, but somehow I found the courage.

We have been through so much so even to this day, we're still in touch, and I have forgiven him. We will always mean something to each other, but we have both moved on. We even talk and laugh during our conversations, but I know that we will never be together again like we were in the past. He has a child with another woman, and I have a child with another man, so there's no way I can deal with that. We actually have turned out to be great friends, but that is where it all ends. Then there was L.A, who happened to be the last boyfriend of my teenage years.

My mind always was racing with new money-making schemes or ideas. I remember as a teenager that I wanted to be a stripper. I figured it was a great way for me to make tons of money in a short time. At that point, I desired smoking weed more than before. I no longer cared about anything I had grown to become numb to the world around me. I had no friends. I could not stand my birth mother for what she had done, and so I resented her greatly. Schooling was something I attempted doing, but I could not focus on my studies. I tried hard to be good at it, but it was impossible. Dealing with depression, living inside of a drug house with frequent police bust really took a toll on me. We had the biggest drug house in Cleveland and Ethel was one of the oldest hustlers. One day our house got raided by the police and they took Ethel to jail for drug possession. Ethel did 18 months and my sister Nita did 3 years in jail, these were the toughest moments in my life. This was another very rough period of my life. Life just wouldn't seem to give me a break!

CHAPTER 3

THE COLD HANDS OF DEATH

After Ethel returned from jail, her health began to slowly deteriorate; she was often sick and was in and out of the hospital. She took terribly sick at some point and it was a major cause of worry for everyone. She was diabetic and didn't help because she couldn't give up alcohol. Ethel got worse and was in a diabetic coma. Her son Mike rang the house one morning; it was Linda that answered the phone.

"Linda, you better come here now, we don't know how much longer momma will be alive for"

I heard him say through the phone. I saw tears flow down Linda's face as she dropped the receiver; I was just standing there transfixed. Could this really be it? Linda walked up to me with tears in her eyes.

"We need to go to the hospital now, Mom isn't doing too well."

Ethel was my angel, and I couldn't imagine life without her. We immediately rushed to the hospital, and it was a sorry and sad sight, it was the first time I was going to see her at the hospital. I still vividly remember her lifeless body there with several machines entering and exiting her different body parts. Tubes were in her nose and mouth and her face was swollen. I wanted so badly to tell her that I loved her one last time, but it was late, she couldn't hear it I held her cold hands and my eyes eased out water. Death had snatched her away from me.

I knew that life as I knew it was over, Ethel had been the one woman who fought to have me when I was rejected by my actual mother. I felt like a part of me was dying too. A big chunk of me had been ripped off.

"I want to die, I want to die!" I repeated over and over. I had no idea, what turn my life would take. Thoughts of suicide filtered through my mind, as I didn't think I'll be able to carry on without her. I could only see dark clouds ahead.

I laid over Ethel's body and crying and Linda had to pull me away. I kept telling God, "You took my angel away."

I would never have known life or love if Ethel hadn't found me. She was everything to me, and I lost her to the cold hands of death. Ethel loved me like her own daughter, fought for me, and wanted me like none other. She was the one person that made me feel wanted and loved, in spite of her shortfalls, she was a decent human. A part of her will always live in my soul and I still miss her terribly. Ethel's loss was one of the hardest pills I ever had to swallow, and my mind was filtering with suicidal thoughts and my days seemed darker, but something kept urging me to go on, and somehow, I kept on.

A mother is truly a gift from God that is instrumental in molding children from birth to maturity. Life without Ethel was really hard; I questioned God and asked him several times why he had to take her away from me. Why he had to take someone who meant so much to me.

In these types of situations everyone always says things like this in hopes to make you feel better, "they're in a better place", "they're watching over you", etc., and it stinks. It's the last thing you want to hear. Don't tell me they're in a better place, because if they were in a better place they'd be here still. A better place couldn't possibly be down in a wooden box six feet under. And I don't want you to tell me they're watching over me, because it's not the same as having them in front of me and hearing their voice or laugh. That's the only way I want them to watch over me. I know these people mean well when they say these things, but it just hurts more to hear.

No one else truly understands what you're going through, which means the people that do understand become so much more important. They are the only people in the world that understand what you have lost, and the weight you now have to carry around with you. Not only that, but you now understood how easy it could be to lose someone because you already lost someone so important to you. It makes you cherish the people you have more than ever before, and it makes you want to hold onto them stronger. The loss demonstrates how important the people in your life are to you. Linda was the next thing I had to a Mother now. And we were both grieving; Linda wasn't taking it well at all.

After losing someone so important to you, you become bitter and resentful towards the world for taking them from you, for robbing you of so much time. You become so pessimistic about life's outcomes. You have to learn to let go of the bitterness. You have to re-teach yourself to think positively, to not always worry and think the worst-case scenarios. You have to learn that this experience does not mean you will never be happy again, and that life will never be good again. You realize that your parent would never want you to go through life with this chip on your shoulder, that they would want you to be happy again. So you have to learn to change your outlook on life, again.

This is the number one thing I took away. Never take a single person, experience, memory, or moment for granted. Everything you currently have can be lost in an instant, without any warning. You learn to appreciate every little good thing in your life and disregard the bad because it's nothing compared to what has been. You have learned what is important in life, and what is not. Your meaning of life has changed forever.

Growing up, I referred to myself as a black queen because I believed I was. Although I was far from perfect because I had already made mistakes and there was going to be even more ahead of me. I just always hope Ethel looks down on me and smiles down at me; I hope to make her proud of the woman I was going to become.

**

When I was fourteen, I started dating a guy named L.A. We started going out together and we spent so much time together that one night I snuck him in my house when everyone was sleeping. We talked a lot that night and ended up having lots of sex. He was crazy about me and was quick to make promises to me, telling me that we were going to be together forever, but I really didn't believe him, I just laughed it off. But soon I started to sense that he was for real and I was falling for him too, just as he was head over heels for me. When he took me to meet his mother, I loved her immediately, because she reminded me of Ethel, her warmth and motherliness got to me. L.A's family were going through a really tough financial period at that time, they really needed help, so I asked Linda if they could come live with us. Linda agreed they could move in upstairs, so I had to fix and clean it up, and they had to pay rent. They moved in a week later.

Linda was gravely affected by Ethel's death also. She started to binge on crack and was abusing several substances. Her excuse was that she was having a hard time since Ethel's death. She said it was awful being sober as it made her cry and remember Ethel too much. So, she took to drugs to help her dull the pain.

Depression soon set in and Linda became excessively negative, only vile and negative words proceeded from her mouth. It was sickening for me. She would curse and swear running in and out of the house. It was as if she was having manic episodes. Her bad habits affected my life as well as I had to sleep during the day as I could not get enough sleep at night. She would get high a lot and come in late at night disturbing everyone's peace.

I got tired of the situation and decided that I needed to leave. I needed to be a strong woman and find my own path; I was tired of the chronic dysfunction. I had no money and no real idea of where I was going or what I was going to do. But I decided that I had enough and I was going to leave. I was going to leave the next day. All I knew was that I needed to find a new shelter, and a petty job to sustain me.

L.A and I got into a fight that night; he must have seen me packing my things, so he knew I was up to something. He was so angry when I told him I wanted to leave. He was angry that I was going to leave him. He shouted at me and threw things around but didn't hit me. He told me he loved me and convinced me to stay with him. I wasn't sure of how much I loved him, he was somehow able to convince me to stay a little longer and promised that things will improve; he promised that we will make it together. I gave in to him, and my first plan for freedom ended.

Living at home with Linda, L.A and his mother was not easy. Linda reminded me of my mother Cece, and it was so sad.

She was always out, and when she came back, she was not herself. L.A tried at first to make things better. He tried to spend more time with me, and sex was all we did all over the house. His Mom was a nice woman and she reminded me of Ethel, but Ethel was irreplaceable in my heart. The only woman who truly cared about me was dead. Linda was on drugs, and I was having sex regularly. I was tired of all of it and wanted a new dimension to life, that's why I wanted to run away.

Linda did try to help me after Ethel passed away, after all, she was the only one I had, and she was my Mother since Ethel passed on. She tried to get me back to school, did my hair and even cooked when she wasn't smoking dope. I couldn't take it anymore so one day I wrote a note, "If you smoke or hit the pipe one more time, I hope you drop dead and never see me again." I left it by her supply of crack and signed my name. I wonder if she saw it, but she never talked to me about it, but she stopped smoking the next day. I praise God that she has been clean since 1999.

My life was purposeless and directionless, I just lived everyday aimlessly. My days were just typically sex drugs and dealing with Linda. I was tired, I was sick of the routine. I wanted a way out so badly, but I felt stuck.

***

Growing up in such dysfunctional setting didn't mean I didn't know what a good family should represent and function like. I believed in the love and bond a family shared. My brother and sister mean the world to me. Although we did not have a lot, we had each other. They were blood and they sure had their own personal issues. Dealing with the hardships of my life made me seek outlets for my feelings. All that mattered to me was making sure my family had food on our table and a roof over our heads no matter the cost.

In April 1994, I was caught stealing at a store. Linda and I were together when a man and a woman approached us. The woman told us that we needed to go with them because I had their merchandise on me. They patted me down and discovered the items I had been attempting to leave the store with. Linda who was also in on it did not get caught. It wasn't my first time doing it, but it was my first time getting caught. I was just seventeen and about to have a juvenile record if I got reported. My whole life flashed in front of me, I didn't want that life for myself. But I was lucky they didn't turn me in. They said since I was honest and had admitted to stealing, they would let me off the hook with a promise that I would never return to the store. I promised I would not, and I thanked them for letting me go. That was the last day I ever use my hands to take anything that was not mine. If I can't afford to pay for it then it's not meant for me to have yet.

CHAPTER 4

MOTHERHOOD AND WOES OF RELATIONSHIPS

When sex was a way of life for me for so many years, it was a miracle that I hadn't ever gotten pregnant. I silently doubted my ability to actually conceive a baby. But that all ended when I found out I was pregnant. My boyfriend initially denied that the child was his; he wasn't man enough to take responsibility. I never considered aborting the baby despite the pressures and challenges at the time. So, in 1994, I gave birth to my child Brittany. And till this day, she stands as one of the greatest miracles in my life.

I won't forget those nine months in a hurry. The thoughts that went through my head. I wondered if I was going to be a good mother, I wondered if I was going to be able to create a better life for my baby than the one I had, I wondered if I was going to show her the love I never received from my mother. These thoughts plagued my mind, but I was determined to see it through.

Every day was a struggle, and I always felt like I had to prove myself to everyone that I was going to be a good mother, that I was ready to face the

challenges ahead regardless of how tough it was going to be. I didn't joke when it came to my daughter and everyone that knew me knew how serious I was about that. I was a fighter, and my every day consisted of fighting and proving to people that I was not to be messed with. If you messed with me, then I made sure you regret ever bothering me, and I made a name for myself like that. I have faced many crises in life as a single mother and trying to be strong and independent was my goal. It was bad for me then but I told myself that I had to take control. I had to take the reins of my life; I was not going down the wrong path in life anymore. I had big dreams and I chose to believe that God had better plans for me.

It was clearly all in God's master plan for me to become a mother. There seems to be no higher love amongst humans than the love of a mother for her child. In the words of Agatha Christie, "*A mother's love for her child is like nothing else in the world. It knows no law, no pity, it dares all things and crushes down remorselessly all that stands in its path.*" This was the kind of love I felt for my daughter.

The bond between mother and child is one of the strongest connections in nature. Romances come and go, but once you've bonded with your baby you're most likely hooked for life. The love you feel for your child is a basic part of your make-up. You're primed to form strong ties with your child. And your child is equally ready to connect with you.

Over the years, scientists and child development experts have studied this phenomenon and have learned fascinating details about the connection between Mother and child. Your bond with your child will metamorphose over the years, but its strength never fades.

I found myself loving my baby before we officially met. I loved her even while she was in my womb. I was hit by a strong mix of emotions and anticipation, and these feelings help set the stage for my relationship with my child. As the weeks went by, the connection felt stronger and stronger.

It was special to spend those nine months of discomfort, pain and physical change with my daughter. My love for her only grew over the years, and I'm always thankful for her. She is special, beautiful, and sweet and has a very kind heart. She keeps me going on my sad days, and together we've been through calm and stormy weathers.

One of our most important jobs as parents is to teach our children the skills they need to become happy, productive adults. There are so many things they need to learn: how to cook, clean, understand finances, get along with others and live with integrity. Our children need us to be very good teachers. And we need to teach them with love and kindness.

Children learn best by example, so it's better to always try to model the behavior we expect of them. They learn from what we do more than what we say. Children love to hear words of encouragement. They like to see you smile, and they want to know that they make you proud. Too much criticism discourages children and makes them want to give up. Focus on their positives and praise them for their progress and their achievements.

Help your child recognize that making mistakes is a part of the learning process. Point out how to recognize the lesson from their experience and encourage them to try again. Remember to *separate the behavior from the child*. Never call them names like "stupid," "lazy," or, "stubborn." Words have great power and impact on children. No wonder the bible says;

"The tongue has the power of life and death,

and those who love it will eat its fruit."

Prov 18:21

My daughter was only a baby when I started making confessions and declarations over her. I would speak blessings over her and tell her she was meant for great and mighty things.

Always be patient with them. If you begin to feel frustrated while teaching a new task, step away. Come back to it when you are feeling less agitated.

One of the best lessons you can give a child is how to love, and you do this by showing the child right from an early age.

"Train up a child in the way he should go:

and when he is old, he will not depart from it."

Prov 22:6

My daughter is and will always remain my best friend and mommy's little angel, I love her so much. I continually tell her that life will be what she makes it. I promise her daily that my struggle will be her strength and I vowed to provide a life for her that was not given to me.

Every child didn't ask to be here, they are innocent, and so as parents, we must try to do whatever it takes to raise our children right. My daughter can always look back and know that I did my best. And my strength has been passed unto her. Today we are best of friends and she can talk to me about anything. Our love and bond will be forever and always.

***

Soon after, the father of my child decided to take responsibility, even though he made me go through a lot. He hustled and tried to provide for us. He actually proved to be a good father during that time. I had given him an ultimatum: either you man up and do what is right or leave us alone for good.

He must have known I was dead serious because that was when he started to show real effort.

It was hard to tell if he did love me. His upbringing probably had its impact on him too. Growing up fatherless made it hard for him to understand how he was really supposed to be a father, or how to love a woman. But this was my excuse for him, I always told myself that it wasn't his fault and he didn't just know better. I always told myself this when I had the urge to leave him.

But he took my love for granted because he felt I was never going to leave him. The journey with him was long and tiresome. Women would come to my house each day to tell me that he had slept with them. Strange women kept calling my phone. Many of these strange women would come to the house too; it was a show at my house on 81st in Cedar every day.

But we had some good times nonetheless, especially on holidays. They were special, like Christmas. He would put us first during those times. We spent a lot of time together, and just cuddle up romantically. One holiday, he even proposed to me with a diamond ring. I was very happy and hoped that maybe there was real hope for us yet. These were the fun memories I held on to in times when I was tired and sick of the relationship. There was more pain than joy. His thinking was very skewed, but in reality, many men do think like this. He would tell me he loved me, and that's all that really mattered, he believed we could have a great life together, but the other women were just his plaything, they meant nothing to him, it was just sex.

It's funny how most men who hold this belief can't take a dose of their own medicine; they won't be open to their partner having an affair but think it's fine that they do. Just trade places and imagine what the verdict will be. What is good for the goose should also be good for the gander.

During pregnancy, child labor was one of the hardest things I had to go through. I had to have a C-section at 17. But that wasn't the real issue. After I gave birth and went home, I had an intense and excruciating pain, this pain was worse than the labor pain, I couldn't move at all. My stomach was constantly twisting and turning, and there was nothing I could do to ease it. I believed it had to do with some complications with the C-section, but how wrong I was. Linda told me this kind of pain was abnormal and that I needed to return to the hospital. Thankfully, I listened to her, so she and her friend Tim carried me and laid me in the car.

After the Doctors examined me, their report was very scary, yet relieving at the same time. The Doctor said if I had been brought in any later, then I might have suffered paralysis in my whole body. My child was born just in time and lucky to escape blindness. I was crying as he told me what the problem was. He said I had gonorrhea, the later stage complications from it, meaning that I had been living with this disease for a long time. But I really didn't notice any funny sign up until after I gave birth. I was curious to understand.

"But Doctor, I didn't observe any strange or funny symptoms, how has this been with me for a long time undetected?" I asked him.

"Most women, about 50% of infected women do show only a few or even no symptoms of gonorrhea at all. Some women suffering from this disease mistaken the symptoms for a mild bladder infection and misdiagnose themselves thinking it's an ordinary urinary tract infection. Moreover, in women, the symptoms are very difficult to identify. But men are almost developing symptoms of gonorrhea swiftly and prominently.

Several areas are affected by infection and it depends upon the nature of contact the person had and period how long he or she had the contact. Generally, the symptoms appear between 2 to 10 days after the infection but in several cases, the delayed symptoms appear even after 30 days after infection. The cervix is the prime organ that is affected in women by this sexually transmitted disease. This can also spread to other parts like uterus and fallopian tube if untreated. So, you see, it really could go undetected in you for a long time. I'm happy you're here now, it could have been worse."

This was confirmation that my boyfriend was a cheat. He was having unprotected sex with multiple women and now transferred this bad disease to me and worse of all risk our child being born blind. As soon as I felt better after receiving medical attention, I wanted to go home. I wanted to tear him apart.

I forgave him and took him back, but it didn't change him, he wasn't a changed man, my low self-esteem made me easily forgive him without any strong commitment to change from him. He was all I knew. I ended up going in and out of the hospital with various kinds of STDs. A part of me wanted to leave, but I foolishly stuck around hoping he'll miraculously change and I just did everything I could to be the woman who would satisfy him all round. I cooked, I cleaned, I was faithful to him, I showed him love in every way I knew how to. But all I got in return was physical abuse, he used to beat me. Looking back, I just yearned so much for acceptance I was going to become a doormat to anyone in the name of love.

We would always argue and fight about his cheating habit. He had a sexual addiction, even if he never admitted, and oh, how I tried to offer myself up even when I wasn't into it for him to do how he pleased, but he'll always still want some other woman. I blamed myself and tried to see what I could do to improve to make him faithful, but the truth is that there was nothing. He was a habitual cheat and even if I looked like the sexiest woman alive, he was still going to go out there and cheat, because he believed he could, and for him, the fun of sex was with having multiple partners.

Like most men who cheat, paranoia sets in when it involves their spouse. He was overly protective of me, and every other guy that talked to me was a problem for him, he believed I wanted to sleep with other men too. He was judging me the way he was. It is true that we see the world the way we are. He thought I was open to cheating too. He was a cheat and he believed that I too would be a cheat, so he was overly suspicious and overly protective. This only made things more heated up between us.

Our sex life was very active nonetheless because I was by now his doormat. One day he beat me so much, he kicked me and hit me in the head, I had black eyes, a swollen jaw, and a bleeding head. He apologized and was pushing for sex that same night. Looking back, if that wasn't abuse, I don't know what is. Another time, he had beaten me so much I had to be rushed to the hospital. I don't know where he got such inkling from, but he was strung out on pills and snuck into the hospital because he thought I was with a guy named Rayvon.

I continued being faithful to him afterward even after swearing to myself that I was going to break up with him, I just didn't seem to be able to stand my ground and make the right decision. L.A soon got arrested and sentenced to a serious jail term. I really felt bad for him and cried. But being alone was a pretty good experience for me, he was away in jail, and I didn't cry or worry as much. Although I missed him, I knew I was better off without him. I realized I was a pretty young woman, I realized I was nice and outgoing, and I was more sociable than I thought. When he was around, I had no social life. I began to realize that I was meant for much more. I was confident I had what it took to make a man happy; this man I had in my life was just unfortunately unable to see my worth.

I was tired of being beaten so much I ended up lying in hospital beds with tubes in my arm, I was tired of being on treatment for STDs. I told myself that enough was enough; I wanted to try and make my life over. I felt like his jail term was God helping me to do that which I couldn't do. I really needed to move on, I deserved better for myself and my baby.

Why did I decide to endure for so long, why didn't I have the strength to leave him? Truth be told, I saw myself as being fulfilled in the relationship, and that I was going to be empty without him, and most women are going through similar situations or feel the same way. I had known him since I was 13, and there's a saying that, "the devil you know is better than the angel you don't know" was my mantra. So I was scared of the unknown, how do I know that the next man out there would be better than L.A? But you see God is always working behind the scenes to make things work out.

I did not have a high school education, and I was on Social Security Income for nine years. It is true that you are the circle you keep, *"show me your friend and I will tell you who you are."* My circle consisted of non achievers, settlers, and people who were not motivated for change; Instead, they hurt people to cover their own pain. As the saying goes, *"hurt people hurt people."* But eventually, you have to start to want more in your life.

Just like the other guys I dated; I always seem to still have contact with them even after we break up. Somehow, we stayed cordial after everything. As I think back on life, I realized that I was bound by fear, and I loved him so much I wanted it to work. But true love isn't burdensome, it heals and doesn't hurt. All I had was the opposite, yet, I hoped against hope that it will work. The fire of the love waned, and it took that separation with him going to jail for me to see. We had been together for 10 years, and all those years clouded my judgment. Today, I still care for him, but separation was the best option for me, I needed to take the reins of my life.

CHAPTER 5

DISCOVERING PURPOSE THROUGH PAIN

Writing this book was really hard for me for many reasons. One of the main reasons I had to get really personal and dig deep into my life is because I know beyond any shadow of doubt that my story will inspire and most likely save lives. Everything I go into detail in throughout this book and the lessons were gained through pragmatic and experimental knowledge.

Placing premium value on your life could really save you from hurt and pain; it took me almost forever to start making the right decisions for my life. Sexually transmitted diseases can carry life-changing consequences. In my case, it could have paralyzed me. It made my body weak. It could have even caused my daughter to be born blind, that thought sickened me. This was all due to the fact that I chose to stick with a man who didn't value me, but more because I didn't place a premium value on myself. He was a man that fed his ego with his ability to sleep with every girl in the hood.

I was deluded that he would get better, but as time went by and I found myself loving him too much and the cycle was never-ending. I was sacrificing so much to keep the relationship afloat. I would make drug runs for him, he would beat me black and blue, I was battling with various STD's, and I started smoking weed again, and I soon even graduated to taking hallucinogenic ecstasy pills. I would often ask myself, "What could I do next to please him?" I was being everything to him. I was the mother, the father, and his lover, all in one. I found myself fighting every day. I gave people a show regularly. I would fight every female that stepped up to my man. I was doing everything to show these women that I had to be respected in my house. Once I ripped off the banister pole to beat someone. I hurt the girl pretty bad, I hit her on her head and she was bleeding, but I didn't stop. Looking back, I was doing everything to protect my territory. All because of his lying and cheating ass.

I was never a follower. I was always the leader. We were a group of girls and we called ourselves 'the Dirty Dolls'. A group of me and six other girls who had each other's back, and no one dared mess with us in the hood. I was a woman that would be down for whatever. I fought people and remember once when L.A had money and lots of it. $10,000 was a lot of money to us at the age of 17. He would come in and say, "Tamika, these niggas are trying to rob me."

He knew he could not tell me anything like that and not expect me to do nothing. One time he got jumped by two guys from another hood. I was ordering my Chinese food when a friend ran in and told me that L.A had got jumped. They hurt him bad, but he did not want to come home because he did not want me to see him in that state. I didn't care; I went to see him nonetheless.

I went to his friend's house that lived behind ours to see him. I made sure he was okay and reassured him that we were going to retaliate. He was going to have to fight them again one on one. And that was exactly what we did. I was aggressive and supportive of him, I would fight for the same man that would beat me to pulp and would cheat on me without thinking twice. I would fight for him without caring about any harm to myself, I didn't have shit to lose, and after all, my self-worth and value were really low.

Men and women alike could learn from my story. I have seen life at its roughest. Pain, despair, and sadness were a constant companion. I have had tubes jammed down my nose, IVs in my arm and so much more. I would foolishly take medicine for these diseases he gave me, but then I would sleep with him before the disease had cleared up. This led to us passing STDs back and forth. How crazy and foolish could I be? I got so tired of laying in the hospital beds. I was being young and dumb.

I remember the times when I would be strong enough to ask him to use a condom when we had sex, when what I really should have done was not allow him to touch me. For crying out loud, it could have been HIV! Men and women get caught up in how good the sex is. No matter how good the sex is, you must still protect yourself, especially when you have doubts about your partner or are well aware of his multiple sex partners. Who knows what the other girls he has sex with are carrying, who knows who the other girls sleep with? Use a condom or walk away! Maintain control over yourself. A moment of pleasure could really ruin your entire life. Just because he/she looks good and healthy does not mean he/she is disease free. Looks could be deceiving. It is real out here in these streets.

If you want to cheat then be real about it. Don't put someone else' life in jeopardy because of your selfishness. Tell the other person you cannot handle being with them alone. I do not recommend sleeping around recklessly. You don't know what he has or what she had before you. In this time and age, people will give you HIV just because they are mad they have it. So it's important to not let love cause you to lose your common sense. Love shouldn't take away your ability to be rational and make rational decisions. But most importantly, you must love yourself first. It's important you love yourself first, even the Bible teaches.

"Love your neighbor as yourself.'

No other commandment is greater than these."

Mark 12:31

You see the bible says, love your neighbor as you love yourself, not more than you love yourself. So, if you love yourself, you won't want your body to be diseased, so why should you foolishly love someone so much that you risk contracting a dangerous disease in the process? Be extra careful. Talk to him or her. Ask how many partners have you had before me? Do you like to be with one woman? Do you like to be with one man? This is just you looking out for yourself, and there's nothing wrong with that. Remember your worth and your value. Don't get into something you cannot handle. I promise you, the Lies, stress, and cheating, would break you and hurt you. You see after one's spiritual life the second most important is your emotional and mental health. Don't let anyone take you for granted, don't let anyone make you feel less than you are.

Men also need to be careful, you can have sex with a woman who looks pretty and slay on the outside but is carrying dangerous STD on the inside. After great sex, you feel a burning sensation when using the restroom. This is when most people end up at the Free Clinic. Then you get the bad news that both of you are sick. I cannot make this any clearer, strap up if you want to mess around. But one woman should be enough if that is the person you have committed yourself to. Please keep those hats on at all times, work it slow, and take it easy.

I had a few female friends while growing up, but as I grew older, it became really hard to keep being friends with females. They were just so much work, many of them were fake. I was very real, and they couldn't understand me. It was a torture to stay in their midst. I still talk to one of the girls from back then, and she was having sex with the whole crew. She had to learn the hard way. I told her she did not want to be considered a "hoe." She was too pretty and worth more than that. I even encouraged her to learn from my situation, but she was enjoying her lifestyle too much to change. Today, she looks back and reflects and the last time we spoke she said "I should have listened to you, Tamika"

***

It wasn't my pleasure to see L.A, go to jail; I was so used to him, despite the constant cycle of hurt. But with time, I started to convince myself that I deserved to be happy. I met a guy named Trayvon, and he asked to be my friend, at the time, I didn't think much of it, so I just said yes. I wouldn't have said yes if L.A was still around but he wasn't and I wanted to explore and see that life could be better than what I had been through. Trayvon promised to be my friend as long as I wanted him to be, and we soon started hanging out for movies, or just eat and chat. One time my car broke down in a blizzard, and he did everything he could to get my car back up and running. He seemed to be a very thoughtful gentleman, and this was really appealing to me. You see, when you've been through so much sadness and pain in relationships, the smallest acts of kindness from a sincere heart can really speak to your heart. I wasn't used to such chivalry.

We got even closer and would spend hours talking on the phone and into the early hours of the morning. I was further drawn to the fact that he was a great listener. I remember when my birthday came; Treyvon had gone all out for me, which was further surprising. I wasn't the kind of girl that was moved by material wealth, and I told Trayvon from the get-go, I wasn't the gold digging type. But he was bent on making a statement there. But I told him I did care about him more than the stuff he gave or could give me. I wasn't after his pocket. He was just a breath of fresh air for me; he treated me like a lady. I needed love and attention which I had lacked all my life. Trayvon asked what I would like for my birthday, and I responded jokingly, "You know diamonds are a girl's best friend."

I told him I was fine with whatever really, roses, cards,

balloons, and the likes. I was just in a happy place at the time, and I didn't care what he gave me, I had never really had a birthday party or a memorable birthday, so I wasn't really big on it.

On my birthday, he took me out to dinner and we went and saw a late movie too. Back at the house, he gave me a beautiful birthday card and balloons. The card read, "Happy Birthday to my wife." And it had $200 in it.

I wasn't moved by the cash, or by what he penned in the card. He called me his wife. Gosh, my heart was melting. He told me that I was different from all the other girls he had been with; he told me that I was a keeper. Let's just say I slept peacefully that night with so much love in my heart.

My affection for Treyvon grew with each passing day, and I started to desire him in every way. I invited him over to my house for a candlelight dinner. I had cooked straight from my heart, and he really enjoyed the food. He was shocked I was able to cook like I did and teased that I should open a restaurant. I had the room set up with a little soft music playing Faith Evans "Never Going to Let You Go." We sat on the bed and started kissing. I was really nervous, but my body wanted it, I craved him. I laid back on the bed, and he took the cue from there and led us into a steamy and passionate rumble in the bed. I could not believe it was happening. I had not been with anyone other than L.A. in ten years; I had not known any other man for that long. I grabbed one of the pillows to put over my face. L.A. was all I had known intimately for so long. I never thought this would happen, yet I couldn't deny I wanted it, I secretly desired it. Trayvon made passionate love to me that night.

Not a day passed by, that he didn't make me feel loved; the sex seemed to put a mark Trayvon was all over me. Eventually, he told me that he loved me; I told him I loved him too. Life seemed bright and fair. We became official on August 1st, 2000. But there was an elephant that we needed to address in the room. L.A was still in jail, and I wanted to go and see him. This made Treyvon nervous and unhappy. He would always ask me, "Will you be going to see L.A in prison?" I never gave him a straightforward answer. But I knew that I needed to go visit L.A. Treyvon and I had the talk, we had to be real with each other. L.A was a man I had spent ten long years with and I couldn't just act like that. I had to at least let him know I had moved on and found someone else. Treyvon was still nervous about the meeting but agreed I had to go nonetheless.

The next month, I scheduled a visit to see L.A. I had to keep it real with him. I was emotional when I saw him; it was hard not to cry. I knew what I was about to tell him was going to hurt him.

"L.A, I've found someone else, I'm sorry, I have to move on," I told him.

I could almost hear his heartbreak as I said the words. He tried to say something, but his lips were just shaking.

"How could you, Tamika, how could you? I love you. Don't hurt me this way," he finally muttered. "Who's the guy? Who's the guy that is stealing you away from me?"

"No one is stealing me away, I just needed to move on, it's hard out there, you know. Treyvon loves me." I told him.

"Treyvon? That dude can't treat you better than me, I know him from the hood. He has fucked around with plenty of girls, that dude can't treat you right, baby, don't do this."

Hearing L.A call another guy out on all the things he himself was notorious for didn't resonate with me. It was just pure jealousy I believed. Even if Trayvon was all that L.A said he was, it wasn't like L.A himself was any different, a case of a kettle calling a pot black.

"Look, Treyvon loves me, and I love him too, he's been there for me, he treats me nice." I told him, "I just came to inform you. L.A."

There was silence for a few moments before he said, "Have you slept with him?"

I didn't want to cause him any more pain, so I lied and answered in the negative, nodding my head furiously as I said no. "Please don't have oral sex with him when you do have sex with him, please," he said as a tear escaped his eye.

It was a strange request, but I couldn't make any promises I wasn't going to keep. I just felt that I owed it to him to inform him. That was all. Funny how he felt bad at the thought of me having sex with another man when I had stayed faithful to him all the years we had been together, and he was the one sleeping around with every girl.

"I'm sorry, L.A," those were my words as I left.

I finally let go of 10 years with L.A. I told Treyvon about the visit and told him I had cut ties with L.A. and he didn't have to worry about sharing his woman with anyone. It was a very emotional decision for me. I was still young trying to grow up.

CHAPTER 6

RECURRING CYCLE

After a year being with Trayvon, I was back where I started. I was honest and loyal to him, I tried everything to prove to be a good woman and partner to him, but that didn't stop him from messing up too. I caught Trayvon at his grandmother's house with a woman in the basement on a blow-up bed. They had on their clothes, but they were cozied up and locked in with each other, embraced, and I could smell sex in the air.

"So this is what I get for everything, Trayvon? This is why you've been ignoring my calls?" I told him and walked back upstairs. Tears streaming down my face, "You can have her Trayvon."

He left the girl on the bed and ran after me, "It's not what you think Mika, I don't have anything to do with that girl, we were just chilling," he said, trying to stop me from leaving.

"You were just chilling? So that's how you chill, right, fucking another girl in your grandma's basement. You're just like every other man."

"Baby I'm sorry, I swear it's not what you think."

"I just can't believe this is what I get after a year of being a good woman to you. To think I really thought you were different, when you're more the same, probably even worse." I told him and stormed out of the house.

Why did it seem that as soon as the relationship got serious and we professed love, everything just went south? I couldn't believe that the same Trayvon who once treated me like a queen will be the same one to hurt me so. I could not believe I had been laying up with this man who always acted like he would never lie or hurt me, only to actually hurt me with spears to my heart. I wonder why he didn't just let me be, why did he chase me so much if he didn't want to be with me? He came back home, made something up, some excuse story and he succeeded in sucking me back in, and I stayed with him. He claimed that he had not had sex with her, that she was just going through a lot and needed someone to talk to, he said he was only being a friend to her and helping her sort out the issues. Even if that didn't explain why she had to spend the night or why they were cuddled up on the blow-up bed, I chose to let it slide. But I started getting emotionally stressed because from then on I couldn't trust him; I was suspicious and paranoid about his every move. The cycle was starting again; stress and pain became my constant emotion. The gash was opened again, and I could feel my heart bleeding again. The relationship was becoming harder than ever for me. This was because I had let my guards down again and trusted Treyvon. My mind was constantly in overdrive, and Trayvon would talk me down whenever I brought up the conversation about us.

Things only got worse as the days passed, Trayvon used to jokingly call me dumb because I used to get SSI. It hurt to hear him call me dumb, even when he would laugh about it, I felt bad nonetheless. If he claimed to love me, why belittle me like that. It was beginning to take a toll on my self-esteem again. I began to feel inadequate and weak, even if I pretended to be bright and happy around him, my internal struggles were major.

Again, I caught him cheating with another girl. Love could really hurt when you give your heart away to people who don't deserve you. Again, I forgave him, but the straw that broke my back was when he ended up in jail for a ticket. I got the call and ran to his rescue. I had no idea there was a surprise waiting for me as I got to the justice center with his mother and my daughter.

To my right where I sat was this lady, and I just didn't know why but I kept looking at her. She must have been there to bail someone too. But I felt funny in my stomach just looking at her. Little did I know my instincts were preparing me for what was to come. I got my paper and left that waiting area, she seemed to be a step ahead of me with the proceedings, so I when I got to the next area she was already there. His Mother and I were waiting for the next step when this woman walks up to us, and looks at Treyvon's Mother, "Hi, how are you? Don't I know you?" She asked.

His Mother just stared at the woman lost, not knowing who she was. His mother looked like she did not know who she was.

"Aren't you Trayvon's Mom?" she continued, to which she nodded in affirmation.

"Don't worry, I got him, you can go." She said to Treyvon's Mom, and then she looked at me and asked, "Are you Treyvon's cousin?"

"No, but who are you?" I asked her back.
Before she could reply, Treyvon was walking towards us, as soon as she saw him, she ran towards him. "Hey honey."

Treyvon brushed her away and walked to meet me, and I confronted him immediately, about who the woman was,

"Just go over to grandma's, I'll explain everything later." He said.

"No, tell me now," I demanded, "Let's leave here and you'll tell me all everything."

"I'm not leaving with you, just do like I tell you, go to my grandma's I'll see you there, I'll explain everything then."

"So, you're going to leave with her? What's this Treyvon? Why are you doing this?"

"Woman do like I tell you," he said and walked away back to her.

I felt instantly humiliated, and I wasn't going to take it, I was going to beat this girl, I charged towards the girl, I wanted to knock her off, but Treyvon interfered, he pushed me against the wall and ordered me to leave. I felt less than nothing. There I was fighting for a man that wouldn't even fight back for me. He was choosing this woman over me and he was so bold about it. I later came to find out that the woman was a stripper; she was an exotic dancer at one of the bars in the hood. I also discovered that she would keep his drugs at her house. I did not allow that, no drugs or paraphernalia was allowed in my house.

I was having a nervous breakdown right after, on the way back home, I was crying so much, and there was nothing his

Mom could say to pacify me. I crashed my car into a tree. My daughter was also in the car. His mother jumped out while the car was still moving, and I blacked out. It happened right on Chester Avenue, it is a large street with 4 lanes of traffic in both directions and there were a lot of cars around. Thank God his mother did not get hit by an oncoming vehicle as she jumped out, and thankfully my daughter was safe too. I started to fall sick constantly. I was sick every day because of the emotional hurt I felt. Emotional pain is worse than physical pain because emotional pain and heartbreak will affect your physical being. I could not listen to any kind of music, if I did, I would break down crying. I was a nervous and an emotional wreck.

I would listen to Trayvon tell me these lies upon lies. The mental abuse was becoming stronger, as he would call me names, even if he was the one in the wrong. Loving him was beginning to hurt too much. He proved to be an unrepentant cheat too as I caught him again with another woman. I was with my dad when it happened. I was driving him to my house, and I spotted him in the car with another woman. I pulled behind him and blew my horn to see what he would do. I had just found my Dad, and we were touching base and trying to get acquainted.

Trayvon kept driving knowing I had seen him, and he ran a couple of red lights in trying to dodge me. I caught up with him when he tried to hide behind a dumpster. I parked behind him, so he could not pull off and I rolled down my window. I looked at him and said,

"I see how it is." Then I drove off. I was just tired. My father told me that I was too pretty to let a man treat me like that. Trayvon turned out to be the player L.A said he was. A relationship that had started out so promising had now hit rock bottom. I wonder why I didn't see these signs before I agreed to be with him. He used to be so kind, gentle and treated me with respect, now it was all disdain, abuse, and disrespect. He used to be away on trips but now we barely spent moments together without arguing or quarreling.

Some men had their way of just making the women in their lives look down on themselves and have their self-esteem debased in the name of love. Most women are taught from when they are girls that a woman's place was in the kitchen and in bed. It doesn't help when they marry controlling men.

One time I called Trayvon out of the blue just during the day to say I missed him and told him I had cooked a special dinner, so I asked if he was coming home. His response, "god damn it, stop calling me about shit like this. I'll come home when I'm ready. If you don't quit messing around, I won't come home. "But why are are you speaking to me like this, what have I done wrong this time?" I kept talking only to find out I was talking to myself, he had long hung up the phone. He was getting into my head in awful ways. My heart was beating so fast, I just went into the room and closed my door, crawled into the bed and cried. I stopped eating, I was vomiting, and I shut my daughter out. I stayed in my room for hours. I sunk into a deep depression and felt like I was worthless and wanted to die. I just wanted to , disappear from earth, I felt useless and unloved. I had confided my life story into this man, and he was treating me like this.

I wondered if I would get over the hurt and pain. I realized how bad the situation was when I found myself in the bathroom and I opened the medicine cabinet and thought, *"They may as well find me dead. I might as well just end my suffering right here."* Tears were flowing down my face as I contemplated taking my life. Either I was going to kill myself, or I was going to kill him. All the negative emotions were flooding into me; I was so stressed and depressed. I kept thinking about all the abuse. I don't know how, but right there in the bathroom, I conceived the idea of getting help, it was like a voice audibly said to me *"Tamika you need help"* I decided to see a counselor. Depression is a terrible thing and remains the leading cause of suicide in the country today. Suicidal thoughts are common, and many people experience them when they are undergoing stress or experiencing depression. The most common situations or life events that might cause suicidal thoughts are grief, sexual abuse, financial problems, remorse, rejection, a relationship breakup, and unemployment. In my case, I seem to have almost all the life events leading up to suicide. I was glad I sought help because I really was this close to ending my life. I had no reason to live, I hated my life, and it was worse that I had nothing or no one to look up to.

When I visited the counselor, I realized who I had become just from answering his questions. I was a woman who was dealing with some serious issues. I saw the counselor about five times, and he decided to give me Zoloft. He said it will make me feel better than I was already feeling. I was told it would lift some of the pressure off of me. I took it for three days, but the side effects were crazy. I started seeing and hearing strange things. It was around this time that I really started seeking God. I believed that I could be healed from depression and its effects on my life. The Doctor couldn't really help; the meds were driving me crazy. I started to pray and ask God for help and miraculously, I was getting better. At this time I found respite in writing down my thoughts and reading the bible.

Trayvon and I were on and off. It's impossible to count the number of times we broke up and got back together. The best thing I found during this period was God, and it was on a personal note, not from being religious or churchy. I found reading the bible therapeutic and healing. Jesus became my best friend. The one who knew all about me and loves me all the same yet loves me too much to leave me the same way. This was where I drew my strength from. I was far from perfect by any stretch of imagination. I had my own personal issues I was struggling with, the main one being anger. But I was getting calmer as I got closer to God and was reading my bible. I remember seeing the verse which says:

Be not quick in your spirit to become angry,

for anger lodges in the heart of fools.

ECC 7:9 ESV

This verse was a deal breaker for me; I didn't want to be labeled a fool, so I made a conscious effort to be less angry.

Now my anger was better managed but it didn't out rightly disappear as I found out one early morning when I got a call from a stripper who bore my name as well. She kept disturbing my phone as early as 7:30 am. I already knew she was trying to get with Trayvon over at my house. Trayvon answered the phone and he hung up after a couple seconds. She kept calling back and wanted to talk to me. I decided to hear what she had to say. She told me how they were still having sex and that he was in a relationship with her, she told me the times he was away, they were together and went on vacations. She was basically trying to get me to understand that they were an item, and I was the intruder.

Calmly I asked her, "What is your point? You are calling here because he is not there with you. You can have him on your time, just stop calling my house."

She then really got me pissed when she asked me why my

daughter was calling him Daddy. I was so pissed that if she was anywhere near me at that moment, I would have hurt her real bad. I was so mad, I hung up the phone. As soon as I hung up the phone, it was a showdown with Trayvon. We got into a serious argument. Just when I was having a good run of calmness, this woman brings her temptation. I was so angry it was hard to keep myself together, I felt like breaking things. I simmered down, ran into my room and prayed to God.

CHAPTER 7

BREAKING FREE

One day Trayvon came to me because he needed my honesty. I couldn't understand why I still cared, I shouldn't have even bat an eyelid when he told me he was going to jail. He asked me what he should do because he was facing serious jail time. He talked to others, but he wanted my opinion.

"Everyone in my family are all fighters, and they're advising I fight the case. But I know you'll give me the best advice. I'm facing a serious jail term at the moment. If I appeal the case and lose, I'll get 15 years, if I accepted a plea deal, I'll get 3 years flat," he told me.

I had tears in my eyes, I really did love him and wished there was a third option.

"I love you Trayvon, and this is a hard pill to swallow, I know everyone wants you to fight the case, but just have it in mind that the chance of you losing will be high, it would make for a good fight if you are confident of victory, but I know you aren't. Three years compared to 15 years is a joke. Don't waste what money you have on Lawyers only to fail. You know how much the crackdown on drugs has been intense lately, how many young dudes in the hood have you seen let off the hook? Please take the plea and do the three years. That's what I'd do Trayvon, I wouldn't risk going to jail for 15 years." I advised him with tears in my eyes, "you're gonna be okay Trayvon."

He started to stress out about setting things right before he had to leave. I told him he needed to own up to what he did and man up. Everyone who sold drugs was aware of the possible consequences of getting caught, 3 years was the best deal I could see out of the situation.

Trayvon was in despair, "Are you saying if you were me you'll just accept and do the 3 years without a fight?"

"Treyvon, just do your time and tell them you are ready to do it now because you have a family you want to come out and be with."

Treyvon couldn't tell me to move on; he was totally confused I could tell.

"Tamika are you going to ride with me?" he asked.

"Yes, why would I leave you?" was my response. Trayvon had tears in his eyes.

"Treyvon, if I ride with you through this you have to promise to be a better man, I'm sick of having to fight for this relationship all by myself, you have to fight with me, you have to promise I won't have to deal with all these other women," I told him.

"I love you Tamika," he said and hugged me tightly. It was a very emotional evening.

Trayvon bought me a car before he went in. He also paid all the bills, bought food and left me some money.

Trayvon ended up in prison in West Virginia. I was upset he didn't spend his last night with me. He claimed to have been sorting out some things. I was the woman he came to for advice and consolation, yet he did not spend the last night with me. His sister and his friend took him down to West Virginia.

I had to learn to grow through the pain. Times ahead were going to be tough. I learned more about the strength that God had put inside of me. Trayvon had helped me with money and groceries, and my general needs, but now all dependence had to be on God. Still, my source of strength was in the word of God.

"And my God will meet all your needs according to the riches of his glory in Christ Jesus."

Philippians 4:19

I continued to stay true to my word to Trayvon, writing him letters and keeping the hope alive. I found further strength in writing poems. It was around that time that I had a look back over at my life and thought, *'why not write a book about your life?"* This was when the project to begin this book was born. God was the source of my strength and the strength of my life. He made a way for me; he kept me strong, his word kept me happy. You see after I thought about writing a book about my life, the devil started to bring doubts into my heart and mind, I began to rationalize and get discouraged even before writing a word of my book.

"You don't know how to write!"

"You are not educated"

"Who cares to listen to what a woman like you has to say?"

"The book is going to fail, why bother writing it?"

These were the lies the devil feed my mind with, and although some of the things were facts, they weren't true. Yes, I wasn't very well educated, but it was a lie that because of that I wasn't going to be able to write my book. Yes, I didn't know how to write, as I had never done anything like it before, but I had written some poems at least. You see there is a difference between facts and Truths. Facts are isolated realities, while Truths are deeper and are a matter of interpreting the facts.

You see, the fact was that I wasn't well educated; the truth was that it really wasn't a stumbling block to prevent me from telling my story. The truth was that I could get an education

enough to write my story, the truth was that I could at least read
and write, so why not tell my story just how I knew how to.

I chose to believe in the truths from God's word. His word which
said,

"I can do all things through him who gives me strength."

Philippians 4:13

Although I was blind to God's love for almost all my life,
I soon began to see the wondrous things he had planned for me. I
found gospel music to also be very healing, and it got me through
really tough times as well.

I got to find out that Trayvon had left some money with
his sister for me. At my age, I didn't see why he had to do that, or
why I had to go ask for something he left for me. His sister and I
decided to ride to West Virginia to see him. And each time we
were supposed to split the gas. I didn't want her saying she did
anything for me. After all, Treyvon was my man. Sometimes I

didn't have my share of the gas money, but I always made sure I sent it to her.

I didn't stop sending Trayvon letters, and my letters were lengthy ones, about 8-10 pages long. Always assuring him of my loyalty and love for him, wishing him well, hoping he took care of himself and that I was waiting on the outside for him. One day as I was riding on a highway to Cleveland and I was listening to Shirley Caesar's "It's my Miracle." Through that song, I had a spiritual experience; it was the first of its kind. The words, "Tamika, it's your day. It's your time," kept ringing audibly. This was the first time I ever felt the spirit of God. I was crying and screaming, "Thank you Lord." I was crying, but they were happy tears.

I went to see Treyvon even in blizzards, and I hate the snow. Five hours is a long drive, especially in snow. I knew he had to feel worse than I did. I'm reminded of the Whitney Houston song, "Count on Me." I believed he was a good man inside, but life and circumstances made him who he had become. He loved his Mom dearly and spent his younger days trying to do everything to make her happy and keep her away from drugs.

On one of the torturous journeys to see him through the blizzards, there was an incidence again with some other woman, a stripper. He was aware that I was coming that day. When I arrived, the other woman was already there. Through all my prior visits I had not encountered this woman. I believed it was the perfect time for it to happen; my response to the situation was strange even to me.

I sat right next to her and politely said, "Hey dear, how are you?" They were both shocked at my disposition, and I said she could stay. Then I told him calmly, "Treyvon, you have to decide today, I can't go through this anymore."

I don't know where I got the calmness from, but it was there, "I'll walk out of here and you'll never see me again, I'll never come back," I told him. I had taken enough, gone through enough, so I was bold in making that assertion. Enough was enough! To my utter surprise, she opted to leave, and she headed back to Cleveland, leaving Trayvon and me.

I traveled to West Virginia smiling and I traveled back to Cleveland smiling too. I wasn't going to allow Trayvon steal my joy. I stopped throwing my love away. It is true that the greatest hurt in the world is love unreturned. My heart is kind and I'll even help a dog. I never once let my history of hurt; pain and abuse determine how I treated others. Everyone needs love, as love is the deepest desire in humans. Crackheads need love, Drug dealers need love, and homeless people need love. I desire to make a difference in the world, starting from those around me. Everything in life happens for a reason, we must always just chose to make the most of situations, especially when they seem dire. A wise man once said, "The difference between a good day and a bad day is your attitude." Choose to make lemonades from the lemons life deals you. I'm reminded of the story about a farmer and his donkey:

One day a farmer's donkey fell into an abandoned well. The animal cried piteously for hours as the farmer tried to figure out what to do. He tried everything he could to get the donkey out to no avail. Finally, he decided the animal was old and the well needed to be covered up anyway; so it just wasn't worth it to him to try to retrieve the donkey. He invited all his neighbors to come over and help him. They each grabbed a shovel and began to shovel dirt into the well. Realizing what was happening, the donkey at first cried and wailed horribly. Then, a few shovelfuls later, he quieted down completely. The donkey had a light bulb idea.

The farmer peered down into the well and was astounded by what he saw. With every shovelful of dirt that hit his back, the donkey was doing something amazing. He would shake it off and take a step up on the new layer of dirt. As the farmer's neighbors continued to shovel dirt on top of the animal, he would shake it off and take a step up. Pretty soon, the donkey stepped up over the edge of the well and trotted off, to the shock and astonishment of all the neighbors.

Life is going to shovel dirt on you, all kinds of dirt. The trick to getting out of the well is to not let it bury you but to shake it off and take a step up. Each of our troubles is a stepping stone. We can get out of the deepest wells just by not stopping, never giving up! Shake it off and take a step up!

God brings people into your life for his specific purposes; some people are for a season, others for a reason. So, don't hold on and cling to relationships that hurt you, never beg anyone to stay in your life. I found a loyal friend in Leslie all through my struggles. Leslie and I became best friends. She will help me when I don't have anything. She would always help and never refuse to do so. She is a great person and a beautiful person inside and out. She's been a rare gift to me through all my challenges. She would push me to do great things. If ever I needed her for any reason, she always came through. She would listen to me and whenever I thanked her she would typically respond, "Don't mention it, what are friends for?" I'm forever grateful for the gift of her friendship.

CHAPTER 8

JOURNEY TO BECOMING

While I was sitting writing this book at my desk, I truly did not recognize my former life anymore. God has stepped in and turned my life around, giving me beauty for ashes and joy for my sadness. Quite literally every aspect of my life has changed for the better. I am finally on my path. I agree I'm not where I want to be yet, but it's more important that I'm not where I used to be. I listened to my inner voice that had been beckoning on me, but had been drowned out, ignored, suppressed and shushed for very long. A path of reaching out to young people, a path of joining, building, and leading communities, a path of open-hearted acceptance for myself and others who had gone through the same, similar or worse situations. I was very much at ease on this path, and well braced for the twists and turns in terms of challenges life would throw my way.

Are you looking to transform your life? Are you ready to follow the path of happiness and fulfillment? Are you ready to commit to this cause wholeheartedly? Here are a few nuggets to help you along the way. These are some of the things that helped me along the way and I trust you'll find them useful on your own journey.

Create a vision for your life: You can never be lost if you don't know where you're going, Hence, you must have a direction. When I wrote out my 10-year vision, I was still struggling to get by, still struggling in abusive relationships and still striving to cater to my daughter. What I'm saying is that I wasn't comfortable when I drew out my vision. There is no better time to start than NOW. A *vision is a clear mental image of the future*. Although I was down in the gutters of life, I stopped feeling that I belonged there. I felt like a chicken, lived like a chicken, ate like a chicken, but I admired to be up in the sky like the eagle, I desired to eat like the eagle, soar like the eagle. There is nothing stopping you right this very moment from creating that clear mental image of what you want your future to be like.

Map out your short-term strategy: The journey of a thousand miles begins with just one step. All great transitions begin with a baby step. Mine was simply cutting off relationships that stressed me and embracing only friends or family that made me happy. I was tired of being tolerated or trying to please everyone with my life. I learned to go where I was celebrated, not where I was tolerated. You see to achieve your vision, you must have a plan or strategy in the short term to slowly lead you into that vision. If you had a vision of eating homemade popcorn tomorrow, you wouldn't just sit back at home thinking of eating the popcorn. You would go out to the market and get some corn, get back home and do the needful. The perfect baby step for me was cutting off unprofitable relationships. Figure out what yours is and take action immediately. It isn't enough to have a vision, you must act, and this is where short-term strategy comes in.

Find Mentors: It was Sir Isaac Newton who said, **"If I have seen further it is by standing on the shoulders of giants."** This was one of the most important aspects of my growth. A mentor can be many things. For some people, a mentor is someone who gives you the occasional useful tip. For others, it's a person who gives you support, knowledge, and encouragement to help you achieve the career of your dreams. Whatever it is you're looking for there are serious benefits in finding someone to help you shortcut the learning process and fast track your career. Experience is not necessarily the best teacher. Learning from the experiences of others, I've found to be a more efficient teacher. A mentor should be someone who has more life experience than you; someone you aspire to be like or who you think shares your morals and values. If you can find the right mentor, you will find yourself receiving an invaluable informal education.

You can have mentors both near and far. Just seek out people who are blazing the trail in your chosen field or career. You MUST have a clear vision in order to choose the right mentor for you. In today's world, there are many motivational speakers active on social media and other platforms. Follow them, read their stories, you will find that there's a plethora of information they have to share. Finding a mentor who you aspire to be like, within your chosen profession also helps you add to your network. It's highly likely that should your mentor not have the answer to a question or problem, then someone they know will. They can introduce you to like-minded people and some of these could be valuable connections throughout your career.

If you have an idea for your business or product then having a mentor to bounce these ideas off of can help you plan and organize how to put them into action and make them a reality. Your mentor may be able to see potential pitfalls and opportunities that had not occurred to you, which could be the difference between success and failure. Motivation can be a hard thing to manufacture but telling your mentor you're going to achieve something and setting yourself a goal means you have someone to hold you accountable to these goals. This means you're more likely to take action and will, therefore, see results quicker.

There's so much more to benefit from having a mentor. It was one of the most important factors that helped turn my life around.

Ignore the Negativity: We all know people who brighten up the room when they walk in. We also know plenty of people who brighten the room when they walk out of it. Negative people can sometimes make even the most positive people think negative thoughts. I don't care if this person is wearing a mask that looks like your best friend or one of your parents, and they tell you they're doing it because they love you. Please ignore them. You won't achieve any success if you listen to the naysayers.

Only a very few people are going to encourage you to change your status quo. Forego security. Fly the coop. Leave the nest. Make a bold move. Usually, they won't encourage you to do it because they've never done it themselves. And that's totally fine! Some of the opposition will be people who do truly care for you and have your best interest at heart. Accept their concern but keep it moving. If they REALLY care, they'll be there to comfort you on dark days as well as to cheer for you when you begin to gain some momentum on your dream-chasing.

Don't ever feel pressured to sit and listen to a negative person. Their negative energy will leak into your own life and affect your attitude. Set boundaries and put some distance between yourself and this individual. If you must be around a negative person, try to keep your interactions to the minimum. Remember, you can't control their negativity, but you can control whether or not you engage. Never allow yourself to fall into the trap of arguing with a negative person, it'll only weaken you and that way you would have allowed them fill your head with even more negativity. Rather than argue, try to ignore any negative comments. Control your emotions and prevent the situation from escalating. Walk away from unnecessary conflict. You'll be respected for taking the high road.

Build a network of positive friends, acquaintances and professional contacts. If someone knows exactly how to get under your skin, you may not be able to manage the situation by yourself. Have the emotional intelligence to recognize when you need help. When you find yourself becoming overly emotional, call a friend or mentor and calmly explain the situation. Oftentimes an objective person can provide you with a different perspective or a new approach.

Negative people aren't just negative to others. They're also negative to themselves. If you already feel negative around them, imagine how they must feel all the time. What are the things the person is good at? What do you like about the person? Recognize the positive things and praise him/her for it. He/she will be surprised at first and might reject the compliment, but on the inside, he/she will feel positive about it. That's the first seed of positivity you're planting in him/her and it'll bloom in the long-term.

Never Give Up: No one said the journey will be easy, but I promise you it will be worth it in the end. You must never give up. Success is sometimes a sum total of all your little efforts put together. Remember that quitters never win and winners never quit, they keep pressing on until they achieve success. If we can overcome the obstacles presented to us and keep pushing through the bad times, we will find the success within ourselves to create something worthwhile.

Even when you think you've done all you can, you're wrong, there's always someone out there who's pushing harder. You don't want to quit, only to realize that you were on the brink of your breakthrough when you threw in the towel. When the going gets tough, the tough gets going.

Remember that we are all human. Realizing that it's okay to make a mistake is only part of the battle to that ultimate goal. Learning and growing are synonymous. Whatever you do, just keep moving forward.

Success isn't rewarding if it comes easy. The real joy of achieving any worthwhile goal is in the process, not in the goal itself. If you want to get to the summit of the mountain, the joy is in the climb, that's what makes making the summit exciting. Every successful person has their story. The secret of their success is in their story, their story makes their success rewarding.

Rome wasn't built in a day, so work towards your goal every day. Victory is just around the corner.

I don't care what anyone says, YOU CAN! Work every day to become the best version of yourself. If Tamika McClain can do it, then YOU CAN do it as well.

CHAPTER 9

TOWARDS THE LIGHT

Trying to cope with a physically abusive partner can be a very difficult experience. Domestic abuse and violence can happen to anyone, yet most people either excuse, deny or overlook the problem. Take it from someone who has suffered all the possible forms of abuse, No circumstance in a relationship justifies abuse of any kind. If you recognize yourself as being either emotionally, mentally or physically abused in your relationship, you need to take action, and take action now!

Physical abuse occurs when one partner in the relationship controls and/or dominates the other through acts of violence, such as emotional abuse (name calling, swearing, threatening, humiliating) and physical abuse (hitting with bare hands or weapons). An abusive partner may hit, kick, bite, hit, spit, throw things, destroy or throw your belongings away. Your partner may also attack you while you're asleep or otherwise catch you by surprise. Your partner may also use a firearm, or other weapons to assault you, abuse or intimidate your family members.

Abuse occurs regardless of culture, education, race, and religion. It takes place in relationships on all economic levels, ethnic backgrounds, and includes all ages. Although abuse could happen to men as well, women are prime targets for abuse. Being perceived as the 'weaker sex' might be at the core of this. Many religions also sideline women and in no way present women as strong characters. I don't care what the excuse might be, but one thing I know for sure is that abusive behavior should never be accepted or tolerated, whether it's from a man to a woman and vice versa. Everyone deserves to be respected, valued and above all else, loved. If you don't feel safe with a spouse in a relationship, then something has to change

Because my story is very personal, and because it's the most prevalent form of abuse, I'll be talking more about abuse to women. Most times, the purpose of the abuse is for the abuser to take or maintain control over their partner. When abuse occurs in a relationship, there is a lack of empathy, compassion, kindness, and obviously, nothing is fair in this love. An abuser will use guilt, fear, intimidation, and shame, as well as physical abuse to wear a victim down and keep them under his control. Sometimes the person may even hurt and threaten the people the victim loves as a means of gaining more power. Whether it be real or imagined.

I'll discuss some of the practical steps and process I went through in order to come out of abuse and to finally be free and self-confident. It's been about a decade now, and I'm living my best life. I'm never going to succumb to any man who doesn't value, appreciate, or celebrate the queen that I am.

I admit it is a difficult subject to tackle, and I've had to dig deep in trying to write this part of the book. My mind had to travel to some dark places. It was a journey trying to analyze my journey towards the light.

Identify the problem: Identify that what you're going through is abuse. The first step to solving any problem is first identifying that there's a problem. If you don't think you're being abused, then you're not. I understand that some women have been so abused they misconstrue abuse for love. I hear from many people who are in abusive relationships, and even those who have left relationships, but say that they love their abusive partner. They wonder, "Why do I love someone who has hurt me so much?" It can feel strange, confusing and even wrong to love someone who has chosen to be abusive. While these feelings can be difficult to understand, they aren't strange and they aren't wrong. Love isn't something that just disappears overnight. It's a connection and emotional attachment that you create with another person. Love comes with a lot of investment of time, energy and trust. It's not easy to just let go of a life you've built with someone, whether they're abusive toward you or not.

With that said, please, understanding that you are being abused opens up the gates to getting out of the situation. Let's call a spade a spade.

Be willful: You do not deserve to be physically abused, or abused in any way for that matter. If you're already in a physically abusive relationship, do not excuse or try to explain the behavior, or blame yourself for it. Do not endure another day. Take a stand! No one can help you if you don't help yourself first. Abuse of any kind is wrong. Be willing to do what it takes to change the way things are. It will be difficult and even frightening. In all abusive situations, change is necessary for your wellbeing your freedom and perhaps your survival. Be courageous. Courage is not the absence of fear, but the triumph over it.

Seek help: It is true that sometimes, we show the greatest strength by asking others for help. This is especially true if you want to reclaim your relationship after being physically abused, you have a lot of work ahead of you. Talk to trusted friends, go to your relatives and seek advice or temporary shelter. Whatever you do, do not make changes on your own. You'll both need help if you still want the relationship with your partner to work. I remember seeking counsel and talking to close friends who encouraged me through different phases of my life.

Turn to God: Living a life of abuse is absolutely not the will of God. It is not something you should endure or deal with no matter what anyone tells you. Abuse is only going to happen as long as you take it and putting a stop to it as quickly as you can is the only way to take control of your own life. Understand that God loves you dearly, and not a hair falls off your head without his knowledge. In telling my story, I remember narrating in an earlier chapter how reading the bible and praying helped to see me through. But I'm about to reveal to you how I found greatest peace and totally had my life back on track. The key is

FORGIVENESS. Yes, you read that right, it's forgiveness. You must forgive your abuser; this is the last piece of the puzzle. I know you are asking yourself, "How can I possibly forgive him after he's hurt me so much?" The way to truly forgive someone is to PRAY for them. Yes, you read that right again, Pray for them. It's inexplicable the kind of peace that comes after doing this consistently.

A quick recap of the points above; identify the problem, be willful, seek help and turn to God. You are the master of your own life. Be strong and courageous. Find solace in the fact that you are not alone. The road ahead won't be easy, but it will be better. Love doesn't include violence and abuse. Don't make excuses for him. Don't highlight one kind gesture, against a hundred unkind ones. Remember to FLY (First Love Yourself); it was my mantra back then. Know that you are valuable and deserve to be loved. Everyone deserves to be loved properly, especially you.

All that I am, I am by the grace of God. His favor and grace have been abundantly and freely given to me. Looking back at how this journey uphill began for me puts smiles on my face. I worked for one week at the Euclid City School as a substitute and I was offered a permanent job afterward.

My supervisor, Vicky had called me to her office. At first, I was nervous, but then she told me that she and others had been watching me work. They were impressed and wanted to offer me a position. They did not want anyone else to snatch me up. She knew I was a good worker. I worked there for three years and praised God for it. It was the beginning of amazing things to come.

After I was confirmed, I knew God was carving out a path for me. When I walked into the building I knew the job was meant for me. Although I couldn't place it at the time, I was positive about it. Later on, I realized God strategically positioned me there so I could help inspire and mentor lots of kids.

It is never too late to dream, I was passionate about taking care of kids and I longed to start a daycare. Only then did I realize that sometimes the past could creep up at unexpected times. I was told that I could not start a daycare because I had a record. It was an assault case from 1999. I didn't know what to do, but I was determined. Someone advised me to go to court and ask for the report and I did. I had to go and appeal it before a judge so that I could qualify for the daycare. I wasn't going to give up easily.

I gave an impassioned speech in the boardroom. I left with a feeling of optimism, knowing I had given all in the pursuit. I could see my speech had an impact on all that listened, as I went through my childhood, and why I wanted to own a daycare. I told them I simply wanted to help little kids and I didn't want my past to deny me that chance. On December 23, 2005, I got a Christmas present in a letter. I opened up the letter, and God had answered my prayer, I became a daycare provider and I've been doing it ever since.

Again I tell you, it's never too late to dream and have a vision. You can go from nothing to something if you never give up. Design a dream and chase it. I never would have thought I would own my own daycare. I never would have thought I would one day publish a book. But here I am today, still dreaming, working on my second book and flowing with business ideas. I'm beyond excited about the future; I wake up each day with a renewed hope and vigor. You can do it as well. You can go from nothing to something too.

I went from living on SSI to earning a proper living. Never be intimidated by the success of people. The Fact That You are HERE Doesn't Mean You Can't Be THERE. The Only Difference Between HERE and THERE Is "T" Which Stands For TIME! Be Patient!

CHAPTER 10

POEMS OF STRENGTH

Here are a few of the poems I wrote through my trying times. I hope you enjoy reading them, and find strength in them as I did and still do.

PAIN

Pain is a part of our existence,
Hurt is a part of our daily life.
How on earth can we avoid pain?
I've had sunshine, now I want rain.

Sometimes, sadness seems unending,
And sorrows a constant companion
What really is the gain?
I feel like I'm going insane.

They say everything gets better with time,
But time must be on a vacation.
Time holds still and I'm frail.
Oh, when again will I sail.

MORE THAN ENOUGH

I've been through the fire
I've been through the flood
I've been through hell and high water
I've been down to nothing
Broke, cold and lonely
Sadness was my one and only

But I know someday I'll have a testimony
When I was down to nothing,
God was up to something
When I was down and out,
God was up and about
When life gets too tough
And living becomes too tough
My God is more than enough.

HURTFUL `WORDS

Sticks and stones may break my bones
But words hurt me even more.
I can heal from wounds and have only scars
But words live with me forever

Hurtful words are like daggers to one's heart
They ruin moods and break lives

Hurtful words are like arrows hitting bull's eye
Leaving people depressed and make them cry.

Why not choose words of kindness over words of slander
Why not choose uplifting words over words that put others down.
For stick and stones may break my bones
But words hurt me even more.

ACKNOWLEDGEMENT

First and foremost thanks to God for his bundle of grace and blessings; also for allowing me to wake up each morning without fear, hesitation or doubt. Like the words of Isaiah 12:2 (NIV) "Surely God is my salvation; I will trust and not be afraid. The lord is my strength and my defense he has become my salvation." All that I am I owe it to God's grace and mercy. All that I am, I am by his grace. Only God could turn the MESS in my life into a MESSAGE, and my TESTS into TESTIMONIES.

Thanks to my daughter Brittany McClain for showing and teaching me what true love is. Because of you I now understand what 'Unconditional Love' truly is. Being your Mother has given me strength and purpose. You are a blessing that changed my whole life, and I look back on the day I bore you with pride and gratitude to God. Watching you grow into the amazing young woman that you are now has been pure joy for me. Keep shining your amazing light baby girl. You make me a proud Mom.

Thanks to my sister Juanita McClain, who showed me love, protection and support in everything I do. Your belief in me astounds me. Your role in my life is a special one; I would never trade you for another. Even though your life story in its own ups and downs, you still remain an inspiration to me. Despite of all you've been through, you still make time to help others. You are a true example of a heart carved in gold. We share a bond nobody can break I love you Nita.

Thanks to my brother Anthony McClain. You always protect me like a father, and I will always appreciate your love and sacrifice. Your outstanding support for my dreams and aspirations will forever be appreciated.

Kera Smith, thank you honey for staying up with your aunt. I'll always love you. You believe in me and I appreciate the help and support you showed me those late nights we shared when the first drafts of this book were being written. Daryl Jr. I love you nephew, and thank you for all the well needed laughs.

To all family and friends, Ruby Keys, Chanelle McCloud, Jennette Bell, Stacey Spears, Gina Spencer, Blinda Jones, Leane Fann, Carla Whitner, Samone White, Catherine Hamilton, Linda Warren, Dorris Warren, Sandra Stanford, Lillard Gardner, Mrs. Harderway, Markita Randel, Sally Larry, Pastor Caver, Sista Caver, Timothy Willis, Lil Reggie, Big Reggie, Jonathan Parries, Marcus Carter, Alexavier Aspen, My father Sylvester Greer , Cecelia Greer, Linda Dennis, Michael Dennis, Andre Williams, Barry Howard, Kennedy, Ivan, Harris

Tim Willis Jr., words won't ever add up to the love we shared. We had our ups and downs, but I Love You to Death. Thanks for your entire love and support king.

Jermaine King (Timothy Willis/ Ougga, I love and miss you Fam) R.I.P my brother/ my best friend, spread your wings and fly king.

Barry Howard, words can't express how you been solid since we met and you don't know how you much you mean the world me. You've been my support team and I thank you and love you for that baby.

Shatina Bryant I wrote my feelings out and you helped my dream come alive. You've always been my favorite cousin even when you were young you always kept your word. I love you so much. Thank you so much. You are a masterpiece.

I can't close this acknowledgement without mentioning Linda Dennis, my mother and friend. Words can't express how much I love you queen. You've been there for me and I'm letting the world know, Hell yeah we been through it but I was the chosen one. You were there when I had my daughter, walking me through the hospital doors and you've been an amazing grandmother to her. I thank God for being the Mother you are to me, and there is not a person alive that can ever take your place. You're an amazing and strong woman and I love you with all my heart. You never left my side through the good, bad and the ugly. You are an integral part of my story. I love you today and forever!

DEDICATION

"Mother Who Raised Me, My Angel Who Left Me"

Ethel Ann Banks

White doves speak of my mother. When I was lost and alone, you found me. When I was cold and hungry you clothed and fed me. When I didn't know how to love, you taught me. Your love for me is unconditional. You are my angel up above.

I consider you my birth mother, you taught me how to be strong but the day God called you home, I felt like my soul left me and I wanted to be at home with you. I still close my eyes and feel the amazing love you had for me. Thank you for raising me the way you did. I no longer question why God took you away because he gave me because I know I'll see you again someday. I love you ma! You will forever be missed.

~~ Tamika McClain

Made in the USA
Columbia, SC
03 November 2020